I0059918

Embracing Success

Through Time Management

Embracing Success
Through Time Management

By

Joy Kelshall

Copyright © Joy Kelshall 2012

All rights reserved. No part of this publication may be reproduced or transmitted in any form or by any means, electronic or mechanical, including photocopy, recording, any information storage or retrieval system, or on the internet, without permission in writing from the publishers.

ISBN: 978-976-8054-91-3

Published by: Joy Kelshall

E-mail: joykelshall@gmail.com

By the same Author: Embracing Success Through Customer Service

Design & Layout by Paria Publishing Company Limited
Cover painting by: Lisa O'Connor
Printed by: Lightning Source

Contents

Dedication

In loving memory of my mother,

Ivy Ramsawak (1929 – 2011)

Her strength of character and fierce determination
encouraged me to always value my time.

Appreciation

I would like to express my sincere thanks to each and every person who contributed towards this manuscript.

Special thanks to my producer, Dominic Besson, for his patience and skill in designing the layout. Thanks also to Cathryn Kelshall for her valuable input and Lisa O'Connor, for her magnificent artwork.

Finally, to my beautiful daughter, Jamie, and my remarkable husband, Lee, I am eternally grateful to them for giving unselfishly of their time to support and encourage me always.

"Time cools, time clarifies; no mood can be maintained quite unaltered through the course of hours." (Mark Twain)

Joy Kelshall

Foreword

This second book by author, Joy Kelshall (the first being "Embracing Success Through Customer Service") is a "must read", as it deals with steps you can take to better manage your time.

Time is a major, finite resource in our lives. You squander it at your risk. Properly managed, it makes life so much better and productive in every way.

We often neglect the proper use of time in our lives and this book will help you correct this and advise on how to do so effectively.

Everyone can benefit from this book's message bearing in mind that *"time lost is never found again".*

Bryan Lee Kelshall

Attorney at Law

X

Introduction

"Every morning you are handed 24 golden hours.
They are one of the few things in this world that you get free of charge.
If you had all the money in the world, you couldn't buy an extra hour.
What will you do with this priceless treasure?"
(Author Unknown)

Why is it that some of us can get much more done in these exact *"24 golden hours"* than others? Considering that one may be more organised or better prepared than the other, it is reasonable to assume that therein lies the answer. However, the solution may not be as simple or as straight forward as this logic suggests.

When I first joined the aviation industry, over thirty years ago, I certainly had to quickly grasp how to maximise every second of each *"golden hour"* if I wanted to enjoy the experience. The airline business is an industry where time plays a crucial and fundamental role, directly influencing its success. It was the very first time in my life I really got a taste of making each moment count. From something as simple as a reserve duty responsibility to the other extreme of operating in an emergency, time was always of the essence.

For example, if I were on a reserve, - which is duty time spent at home, - the company could call me by telephone, at anytime during this particular defined period, to operate any international flight. I then had a maximum time of 60 minutes to be ready for a *"pick-up"* to report for duty or face the consequences. Not an easy feat by any means - I can assure you - if I was totally unprepared. On the other hand, in an emergency situation we were trained to evacuate the passengers on the aircraft in ninety seconds using only half of the available exits. I was never so grateful for this demanding, time-focused training drill until the day we actually had to put it into practice. On that eventful day, I gained a renewed value for time which is forever stamped in my memory.

In our daily lives many of us become fantastic jugglers coping with time issues. How best then can we get a firm grip on what works best? We must not kid ourselves into believing that time management is simply about how well we handle ourselves on any given day. The management of our time on that particular day will absolutely affect the outcome of what happens in the following day(s). A simple analogy is to imagine you are planting a garden. Long before the garden can mature and the flowers bloom will be the effort you have to put into growing them. The more you invest in nurturing a healthy garden,

the better the results. It is the same concept with time, the more you invest in managing yourself today, the more time you will have to ensure a balanced, well-adjusted existence on the morrow. Therefore I want to encourage you to not only think of time management as effectively dealing with a daily series of tasks and events. I want you to treat with it as an on-going, never-ending lifestyle which will be reflected in how you unswervingly behave to maximise your time. M. Scott Peck said, *"Until you value yourself, you won't value your time. Until you value your time, you will not do anything with it".*

The answer I believe, to be able to effectively and efficiently manage time, is dependent to a large extent on how you **consistently** manage your life. It involves your attitude and habits which will directly affect your ability to succeed. The only way forward is to plan ahead. You ought to know what you want in life. You should then design a course of action which will help you get what you want. To a lesser degree, successful time management also depends on the tool you use. This tool is the system or method that works for you personally and may or may not be what works for others. Whether it is a *"things to do list"* or an electronic organiser, most of us would probably choose the most comfortable and user-friendly system that allows us to effectively manage our personal time, whether at work, at home or at play. I believe that, in a nutshell, time management is simply a way of life. Well known author on personal time management, Alan Lakein wrote, *"Time = life; therefore, waste your time and waste of your life, or master your time and master your life".*

The purpose of this book is to explore the concept that successful time management is simply a way of life – a continuous process of planning and organising ourselves. This will include identifying and dealing promptly with matters so as to eliminate interruptions and time wasters and also learning how to successfully plan, prioritise and delegate tasks. In addition, we will revisit various proven systems of time management, in order to decide which one provides us with a personal best fit. The recipe, however, to embracing personal success through time management is to further examine our habits and attitudes to discover how we manage ourselves and why we may have problems with effectively managing our time.

I have chosen to write this manuscript in a workbook format. This design is to assist in your participation, involvement and use of **time**. I have drawn from my personal experiences especially in the airline industry to reinforce the importance of you treating your time as simply a way of life so that you can embrace success.

After reading this book you will be able to:

- Define time management and be better able to improve your time management skills

- Identify various established systems of time management and choose the one which is ideal for you

- Analyse problems that arise with regard to one's attitude and habits

- Plan and prioritise tasks

- Identify time wasters and learn how to eliminate them

- Better understand how to successfully delegate

- Communicate more effectively

- Acknowledge the benefits of successful time management

- Better manage yourself and time

"Being rich is having money; being wealthy is having time."
(Margaret Bonnano)

Chapter 1

What is Time Management?

"Make use of time, let not advantage slip."
(William Shakespeare)

"I need more time!" Many of us frequently find ourselves in situations where we always seem to have too much to do and too little time to do it. Ideally, we all want to have enough time to do whatever we have to do, with extra time left to spare for the other things that crop up. So how do we get to that perfect place? Finding the most suitable definition for time management is a good place to start. How would you personally describe it?

Write a simple explanation of *"Time Management"*.

_____
_____
_____
_____

Some experts have defined time management as:

- *"A system for controlling and using time as efficiently as possible"*

- *"The ability to manage yourself within a given time"*

- *"Really a misnomer - the challenge is not to manage time, but to manage ourselves"*

- *"Managing yourself to get your specific task done in the time you allocated"*

- *"The development of a process and tools that help you be more productive and efficient"*

- *Time management is simply a way of life.*

After reviewing the above and many others, when you think about time management, you realise it is much more than making sure that you get things done within a specific time frame. Effective time management works in concert with how you manage your daily life. You do not wake up one morning and tell yourself that today is the day you will get it right. You have to develop healthy habits and an optimistic attitude to be able to, day in and day out, organise yourself to cope with whatever expected and unexpected events occur. This means that you would display how you control your time and life by the choices you make. Certainly, other factors will influence your decisions, but each of us gets to decide how to respond to these, and how to shape and mold our individual lives.

I can recall operating a flight from Antigua to Miami which had a flying time of approximately two hours and forty-five minutes. During this time, the passengers were to be offered drinks and a hot meal. To be able to accomplish this on time, before wheeling the bar trolleys out, the ovens had to be turned on for thirty minutes to heat the meals. That day a cabin attendant, who always appeared to be *"very laid back"* and *"super cool"*, was designated galley duties. This meant that it was her responsibility to turn on the ovens. However she carelessly *"forgot"* to turn them on and this resulted in all of us scrambling to ensure that we served the meals and cleared the trays before we landed. I don't have to describe the sloppy service we meted out to the passengers that day. All because she failed to organise herself and plan ahead, and those thirty minutes we lost, could never be regained.

To get a better handle on your time you need to adopt a constructive attitude to how you manage your life. You also have to be able to accept total responsibility for all your actions. This involves looking into the future and preparing for upcoming events. Stephen Covey, in his book, *"Seven Habits of Highly Effective People"* explained it beautifully, when he wrote, *"Begin with the end in mind"*. In other words, set your goals and work towards them. Only then will you begin to see new alternatives and possibilities that will create more time. Ultimately, your personal success in managing your time is all up to you.

The following self assessment will help you to determine how well you presently control/manage your time.

Time management self-assessment

Circle "YES" or "NO" to answer the questions below.

1. Are you always on time for work? (YES/NO)
2. Are you always on time for social occasions?
    (YES/NO)
3. Do you complete your work and chores on time?
    (YES/NO)
4. Can you find everything you need quickly?
    (YES/NO)
5. Do you usually leave work on time? (YES/NO)
6. Do you have enough time for your family and friends?
    (YES/NO)
7. Do you feel in control of your life? (YES/NO)

There is an old Chinese proverb which says that *"no amount of gold will buy you time that has passed".* If you take into account, that any time squandered can never be recovered, it will therefore, be in your best interest to not fritter away a single second of such a precious commodity.

"Dost thou love life? Then do not squander time,
for that's the stuff life is made of."
(Benjamin Franklin)

Chapter 2

Systems of Time # 1
"Reminders"

"A schedule defends from
chaos and whim."
(Annie Dillard)

Over the years many have tried to perfect time management skills. Results from surveys and research have put some of these improvements into four systems or *"generations of time management".* These are:

1. *"Reminders"*

2. *"Planning and preparation"*

3. *"Planning, prioritising and controlling"*

4. *"Planning, prioritising, controlling, plus the importance factor"*

1 "REMINDERS"

In straightforward terms, this *"reminder"* is based on a list of things to do. This listing helps you to focus on the errands and tasks you have to do. You write things down; check them off as you complete them and you are good to go. E.g. Make an appointment or pick up your dry cleaning, etc. The difficulty with this method is you have no real structure of timing to complete the listed items. You do check

your list from time to time but you tend to do what is in front of you and then deal with their consequences. In addition, if you forget to look at your list, chances are you will fail to remember to do some of the tasks you wrote. This can have a negative effect, not only on you, but also on other people. If your neglect leads to broken promises to others, then you may jeopardise your relationship with them.

A *"things to do list"* can be pretty effective, but you must be aware of its constraints to be able to maximise its capabilities. I would suggest that if you were to use a *"things to do list",* you actively treat with it as you would a checklist. In the aviation industry the pilots, to avoid mistakes, use a checklist which is a mandatory requirement for every take-off and landing. In the cabin, we also used a checklist to check emergency equipment, catering etc. and I can assure you the only way it worked was to physically use it and not rely on memory – even if you truly believed that you could. During classroom training sessions I reinforced and emphasised this to cabin crew repeatedly, in an effort to encourage them to consistently practice it. Business consultant, Dr. Claudia Stein said, *"It (the checklist) helps companies develop the critical steps necessary (to plan). Businesses have fire plans and contingency plans. This is just another tool they need in the workplace".* A checklist requires a tangible response which would ensure that you remember all that is written on it to enable you to move on to the action step.

Design your own checklist with the things you need to do every morning before you leave for work. Begin to physically use it to get you started in developing a new habit.

"You might well remember that nothing can bring you success but yourself."
(Napoleon Hill)

Chapter 3

Systems of Time #2
"Planning and Preparation"

*"By failing to prepare,
you are preparing to fail."*
(Benjamin Franklin)

#2 "PLANNING AND PREPARATION"

To improve on the timing aspect of *"reminders"*, personal goals were introduced together with calendars and appointment books in the second system of *"planning and preparation"*. It was believed that this upgrade would help to meet obligations and be more responsible since you now had a prepared schedule to rely on. However the down side of this process was that one was inclined to focus more on the schedule than people. In other words, sticking to what was listed in your calendar and appointment book became more important and people turned into impediments. As effective as this development was, even though one got a lot more of the tasks done with a schedule, you now needed much more time to muddle through time consuming relationship issues, which were then created, having ignored other people.

During the time I worked as a flight attendant, we sometimes had to operate flights with a minimum of crew members. Nonetheless, we were expected to maintain the same level of excellent service. But with the added tasks, it was tempting for us to put on blinkers when walking up and down the aisles thereby avoiding eye contact or activated call buttons of passengers. Except inevitably, if we succumbed to this inducement it usually ended with us having to spend more time pacifying the now annoyed passengers. It would have been better to immediately acknowledge them and their requests. We may not have been able to deliver right away but in the long run we would have saved time by avoiding the confrontational issues which arose because of our inattention.

If you use a schedule as the tool to *"plan and prepare"*, be mindful that when people get in the way you cannot shut them out like you would a planner, by closing it. A schedule/plan is a useful mechanism to help you get more things done while aiming to reach your goals. First and foremost though, you must remember that *"no man is an island"*, and you will always need cordial relationships to successfully maximise your time while attaining your goals.

Take some time now to identify and list three personal goals. Earl Nightingale, one of the world's foremost experts on success and what makes people successful, wrote, *"People with goals succeed because they know where they're going"*. Remember to use the **"SMART"** mnemonic when doing so to ensure that they are:

S –   **Specific** – You need to know exactly why you want to achieve this goal and what you have to do to get it. After all, the more you understand the easier it is to make time management decisions.

M –   **Measureable** – Goals or objectives must be stated in quantitative terms e.g. in the airline, for each passenger who arrives at the check-in counter, a specific time frame is assigned to the process to ensure that the transaction is completed efficiently and effectively. The airline representative is required to complete this task, in the defined time frame to ensure the flight departs on-time. So too, your goals should have enough details for you to measure your performance and make it easier for you to judge your success or failure.

A –   **Attainable** – This simply means that your goals must be reasonably within your reach.

R –   **Realistic** – Goals must not be *"pie in the sky"*. They must be down-to-earth and practical. Use your available resources to reach your goals. Remember time is a resource also.

T –   **Timed** – Target dates to complete your tasks so as to achieve your goals. This creates a path and direction as you pursue and enhance your management of time.

Research has also improved on the SMART mnemonic by not only adding new words to each letter but also by extending the mnemonic from SMART to SMARTER.

Wikipedia has the following table:

LETTER	MAJOR TERM	MINOR TERMS
S	Specific	Significant; Stretching; Simple
M	Measurable	Meaningful; Motivational; Manageable
A	Attainable	Appropriate; Achievable; Agreed; Aligned
R	Relevant	Realistic; Results-orientated; rewarding
T	Time Bound	Tangible; Timely; Time-orientated
E	Evaluate	Ethical; Excitable; Enjoyable; Engaging
R	Reevaluate	Rewarded; Recorded; Reaching

The additional E and the R are pertinent because we all have to deal with the many changes and unplanned events that occur. It will then obviously be useful to reconsider our original goals in order for us to redo them if necessary. If you want to also add more words to those above, please do so.

Goals:

1. _____

   _____

2. _____

   _____

3. _____

   _____

Intrinsic to success and attaining your goals is an investment in, not only time, but also in relationships.

"A man who does not plan long ahead will find trouble at his door."
(Confucius)

Chapter 4

Systems of Time #3

"Planning, Prioritising and Controlling"

#3 "PLANNING, PRIORITISING AND CONTROLLING"

*"One always has time enough, if
one will apply it well."*
(Johann Wolfgang von Goethe)

The third system consisted of *"planning, prioritising and controlling"*. It focused on adding direction and orderliness in what to do and how to do things. This system also linked personal goals to personal values. In an effort to build on competence and reinforce skills, it initiated the use of modern technological aids like electronic organisers and computers. But the effort to *"plan it, schedule it and manage it",* can result in the control aspect of this system taking precedence over everything else. One can literally become a *"control freak".* By only using this system; you may forget that even though you can control the choices you make, you cannot control their outcomes. You cannot also dominate the people you continue to share this planet with. This approach works because there is an increase in your efficiency and productivity on one hand, but on the other, you also become less effective since your focus is on how *"to do things right"* and they may not necessarily be the *"right things to do"*.

In effect, you try to impose your personal values on others as being *"right"*, and these values may mean absolutely nothing to them. For example, you may believe that no one can be happy unless they own a big house and it is super important to you to be considered well-to-do. Except not everyone feels that way. Others are perfectly happy to settle for a smaller house and being wealthy means something else to them. American senator, John Kerry, defined values as *"Values are not just words, values are what we live by. They're about the causes that we champion and the people we fight for."* Because of these varied values in dealing with people one is unable to always predict how much time should be allotted to them. This is never an open and shut case since individuals will understand and internalise things using many different methods and time frames. I remember having to train new recruits on board the aircraft and each and every one of them had to be managed differently to achieve success. Mind you, the content and information were the same; however, some needed more attention to understand while others *"breezed"* through.

Even though it is great to be efficient, the method of planning, prioritising and controlling, is certainly not enough. You need to be constantly aware, when using this method, that your values are not the same as others and this should be accepted and respected. Therefore you should allow yourself to be flexible and ready to adapt to change and to devote as much time to individuals as they each require. Being competent only, is not enough; caring, patience, sensitivity to others and an open mind is essential to flourish and arrive at a successful balanced existence.

What are your values? Record at least five of them.

Values:

1. _____
   _____
   _____

2. _____
   _____
   _____

3. _____
   _____
   _____

4. _____
   _____
   _____

5. _____
   _____
   _____

"Not everything that can be counted
counts, and not everything that counts
can be counted."
(Albert Einstein)

Chapter 5

Systems of Time #4

"Planning, Prioritising, Controlling, and the "Importance" Factor"

"The bad news is time flies. The good news is you're the pilot."
(Michael Althsuler)

#4 "PLANNING, PRIORITISING, CONTROLLING, AND THE "IMPORTANCE" FACTOR"

This fourth practice combined the positive features of the above three systems, removed the flaws and then added the *"importance"* factor. This means that the spotlight is now more on what you do and why you are doing it, rather than how quickly you can get it done. In other words, you concentrate first on *"doing the right things"* as opposed to *"doing things right"*. This approach allows you to focus on developing better relationships with people, thereby encouraging mutual respect and trust. It actually helps you to strike a balance between your working life and your social life. It involves your total

commitment and the outcome is your personal growth. Because you have also put more effort into enjoying leisure time, you can return to the workplace with a positive attitude, enabling you to work more efficiently and effectively – thereby maximising time.

This system actually differentiates between the *"urgent"* and *"important"* things we do. It requires us to cultivate a distinctive way of thinking before we act so helping us to make our final decisions. Many of us can get confused with whether something needs to be done right now or not - whether it is *"urgent"* or *"important"*. For example, traffic congestion on the roads puts us in a heightened sense of anxiety echoing that we will be late in arriving at our destinations. This emotional upheaval will certainly affect how we continue to behave. Some of us are always in a tailspin rushing to meet deadlines and commitments without ever stopping to ask ourselves if they are really necessary. In reality by reacting in this manner to various situations, we are allowing the commotion of these perceived, demanding issues to affect the choices we make.

Hold on, I am not saying that there is never a need to rush to do things at times. Occasions will occur which will demand this reaction. The problem begins when we rush all the time and never separate the things that are actually more important from those that are not. The more we make things to be of great importance, the less significant they can become. Former Prime Minister of Australia, Robert James Lee (Bob) Hawke said, *"The things which are most important don't always scream the loudest"*. This *"importance"* factor works jointly with planning, prioritising and controlling for us to succeed. It is the main ingredient in this model which allows us to maintain personal equilibrium, enjoy peace of mind, and invest in spending quality time.

Even though we usually react involuntarily to perceived emergencies, be that as it may, it is not always necessary to spend as much time there as we do. A good idea is to take ourselves out of a given scenario and instead of asking what do we do, ask ourselves, *"What is going on here?"* We used this approach when faced with an emergency situation during flights, and it gave us time to focus, better evaluate the situation, and so be able to prioritise more effectively. The tendency to instinctively panic can negatively affect the decisions we make. It compromises not only the given time needed, but also how to most effectively respond. If, however, one has to be personally successful in managing time, you must first control your subjective reaction to situations and adopt an objective attitude to be able to make the right choices. These choices will ensure that you are doing the right things and they will create more time for you to effectively handle any given circumstance the right way.

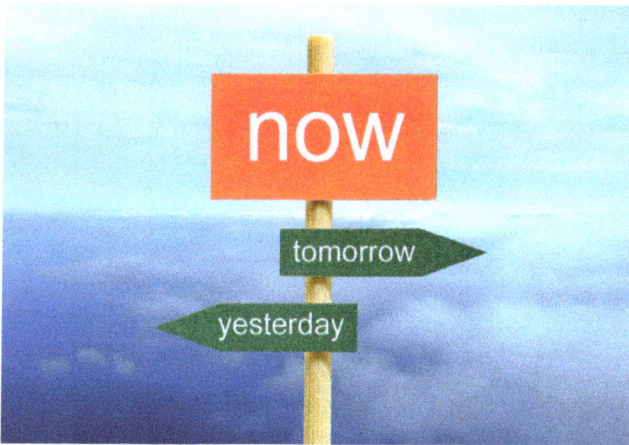

"The key is not to prioritise what's on your
schedule, but to schedule your priorities."
(Stephen Covey)

Chapter 6

The "Importance" Factor

"Time is very slow for those who wait; very fast
for those who are scared; very long for those who
lament; very short for those who celebrate; But
for those who love time is eternal."
(William Shakespeare)

The "Importance" Factor

Have you ever noticed how quickly the time flies
when you are having fun? Alternatively, doesn't it drag
when you are stuck doing something that is pretty
mundane? I can pleasantly reflect on the fun we had in
London during the layover time we spent there as airline
crew. The Latin expression *"tempus fugit"* meaning *"time*

flees", or more commonly *"time flies"*, comes automatically to mind with this memory. However, getting to London always seemed to take forever, especially as it was a night flight and we were not allowed to sleep for obvious reasons. Those nights passed at a snail's pace and it was usually a struggle to stay awake even if we had taken an early afternoon nap prior to operating the flight.

Despite the monotony we can do most routine tasks automatically. Conversely, important things like people and relationships require more than a mindless reaction. They actually require us to make a conscious and deliberate effort. The importance we place on others' needs will be reflected by the amount of time we devote to meeting them. Stephen Covey wrote, *"Little kindness and courtesies are so important. In relationships the little things are the big things"*. Complete the following table by answering the following.

1. Make a list of five things that matter to you.

2. Prioritise this list by numbering them, with the most significant thing listed as number one.

3. Next to each item, write how much time you genuinely spend there.

Things that matter to you	Prioritise your list	How much time spent there?	Why is this so?
1.			
2.			
3.			
4.			
5.			

If you are not spending as much time as you should in an area that is more important to you than others, ask yourself why this is so.

It is inevitable that after this exercise many of us realise that as important as our health is to us, we do not make enough time to physically exercise. As important as our spiritual life is to us, we somehow do not take enough time to feed our soul. As important as our family and our friends are, we never have enough time for them. The list goes on…. What a wakeup call this can be!

"I must govern the clock, not be governed by it."
(Golda Meir)

Chapter 7

Choosing What Works For You

Choosing what works for you

"Life is the sum of all your choices."
(Albert Camus)

Each of these four systems of time management from the previous chapters has both positive and negative elements. You may choose to adopt one style and others may opt to take another. Some people may choose to take specific parts of some, put them together and form a method unique to them. Whatever system you choose to use remember to include the *"importance"* factor. Successful personal time management is simply a way of life and it depends on you being totally responsible for yourself. So choose which works best for you, add the *"importance"* element and enjoy the benefit of having available extra time. Robert Fritz, author, composer, film-maker and management consultant wrote, *"If you limit your choices only to what seems possible or reasonable, you disconnect yourself from what you truly want, and all*

that is left is compromise". The ball is in your court for you to apply the strokes required to achieve your personal goals with the additional space on hand to enjoy good relations with others.

Recap

If you want to embrace successful time management and have the time for those very important things in your life, you will have to:

Acknowledge the most important things in your life. (List your 5)

_____

_____

_____

_____

_____

_____

_____

_____

_____

_____

⏰ Maintain a positive attitude towards improving how you control your time, to have enough time for these important things. (List changes you will have to make regarding these 5)

_____
_____
_____
_____
_____
_____
_____

⏰ You may have to change old habits and adopt new ones. (List the old & new habits)

_____
_____
_____
_____
_____
_____
_____
_____

⏰ With regard to work, you will have to examine if there is a need to restructure your schedule. (List changes)

_____
_____
_____
_____
_____
_____

Much like the garden I mentioned earlier, you will have to continue planting, cultivating and watering the important things in your life. This will allow you more time to spend on issues that are important to you. A *"tool"* will not manufacture the fundamental changes in the results we want in life, but by concentrating on the important issues to improve the quality of our lives, this will result in the changes we wish to get.

"In the long run, we shape our lives, and we shape ourselves. The process never ends until we die. And the choices we make are ultimately our own responsibility."
(Eleanor Roosevelt)

Chapter 8

Healthy Habits

*"Bad habits are like a comfortable bed;
easy to get into, but hard to get out of."*
(Unknown)

Healthy Habits

Exactly what is a habit?

According to Wikipedia,

"Habits are automatic routines of behavior that are repeated regularly, without thinking. They are learned, not instinctive, human behaviors that occur automatically, without the explicit contemporaneous intention of the person."

Another definition is: *"an established custom"*.

How would you define it?

_____
_____
_____
_____
_____

I like to think of habits as shifting into autopilot. I recall during flights, especially lengthy ones, the pilots would sometimes let the aircraft fly on autopilot. This meant that the aircraft was literally flying itself with no help from the pilots. It is a perfectly normal and legal action which is meant to assist pilots. In our daily lives, when we operate on autopilot we are acting by rote without consciously having to think our actions through. For example, for every take off and landing we sat on our jump seats and buckled up to protect ourselves. This did not require much thinking or any specific attention; it was what we did instinctively and was required of us to do.

Think of the many actions we practice daily, for example like having breakfast or lunch, getting dressed for work or driving our cars. We develop *"good"* habits of setting the alarm clocks to avoid being late or using seatbelts when we drive. Alternatively some of us have *"bad"* habits, like not using alarm clocks or driving without seatbelts. The consequences of these *"good"* habits may be a promotion at work or to reach our destinations safely. On the contrary, *"bad"* habits can result in being fired or getting hurt in traffic accidents. Warren Buffet said that, *"Bad habits are like chains that are too light to feel until they are too heavy to carry"*. If we persist in our *"bad"* habits we can certainly get bogged down, constantly rushing to complete what we started out to do.

Examine the flow of sequence below:

Mad rush to complete task → Awakes late & panics → Arrives late & flustered → Misses appointment → Deals with angry boss → (Mad rush to complete task)

You fill in your own sequence with a reoccurring event (habit).

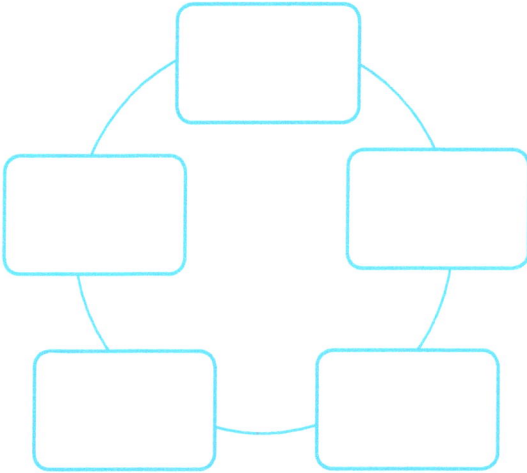

Can you change this?

The ability to take over from autopilot and personally steer your life requires that you take responsibility for you. Easier said than done!! It will definitely not be easy to do since it takes a limited time to create a habit and a much longer time to break it. A good idea is to devise a workable personal plan. Either you post sticky notes everywhere to remind you, or you enlist the help of family and friends to *"be on your case"*. Whatever you do, remember to take *"baby steps"* on changing and refuse to accept defeat. After all, it will not be long before you would have acquired a *"good"* habit which would act as an efficient and effective guidance system whenever you need to *"switch on the autopilot"*.

List as many habits you can think of. Sort them into the two columns below as *"good"* or *"bad"* habits. With regard to the *"bad"* habits, number them with number one being the first one you will work on etc. The only way to win is to tackle them one by one. After your first victory, the others will become much easier.

"GOOD" HABITS	*"BAD"* HABITS

Research records, *"As behaviors are repeated in consistent settings they then begin to proceed more efficiently and with less thought as control of the behavior transfers to cues in the environment that activate an automatic response - a habit."*

"Habit is habit and not to be flung out of the window by any man, but coaxed downstairs a step at a time."
(Mark Twain)

Chapter 9

Attitude

"If you are going to achieve excellence in big things, you develop the habit in little matters. Excellence is not an exception, it is a prevailing attitude."

(Colin Powell)

Attitude

Winston Churchill once said that *"attitude is a little thing that makes a big difference"*. A sentiment I fully endorse. If you buy into the concept that time management is simply a way of life, then your attitude would automatically support this. In my book, *"Embracing Success through Customer Service"* I used the analogy of a glass with some water and asked the aged, old, familiar question, *"Is this glass of water half-full or half-empty?"* I explained that the answer of a half-empty glass conveyed a pessimistic attitude, in that the focus is on what is lacking in life, with the negative belief that things will worsen. However the response of a half-full glass reflected an optimistic and positive attitude dwelling on the good things in life, with high hopes of them getting better. In other words, a half-empty glass meant that the water will continue to lessen and eventually disappear. Alternatively, with a half-full glass, the water will continue to rise to the top and overflow. Your attitude will determine how you see the water in the glass.

Your attitude works like a sieve and this affects not only how you see things but also what happens to you. An optimistic attitude will help you to build your resilience. This means that when faced with unexpected events or changes you are able to manage them effectively. In addition this positive attitude will allow you to be more enthusiastic and energetic about what you do. This causes others to respond likewise and helps you to build successful relationships. People really like being around a confident and happy person. A pessimistic attitude leads to an unhappy and unrewarding lifestyle and helps to drive people away from you.

I found this slide on the internet which says it all.

ABCDEFGHIJKLMNOPQRSTUVWXYZ
1234567891011121314151617181920212223242526
Attitude is Everything!

❏ A = 01
❏ T = 20
❏ T = 20
❏ I = 09
❏ T = 20
❏ U= 21
❏ D= 04
❏ E = 05

_____
100 %
_____

Customer service
Excellent ✓
Poor ☐

❏ Your attitude determines 100% of the impression you leave with people everyday.

THE GOOD NEWS

❏ You Get To Choose Your Attitude!

A positive attitude is the key to changing your habits. When you realise that you have to consistently work on creating new habits, it is this attitude which will determine your success. It is President Abraham Lincoln who said, *"Always bear in mind that your own resolution to succeed is more important than any other one thing".* Habits and attitudes are intricately linked together and a positive attitude will guarantee *"good"* habits. This will in turn allow you to have all the time you need to become successful.

Research maintains that *"it is not what happens to you, what counts it is how you react to it."* It also says that a positive attitude improves your health, and besides being infectious, gives you a better chance to succeed. How then can you change a negative attitude to a positive one? Study recommends that whenever you get a negative thought you try to replace it with a positive thought. Not an easy task by any means but, if you think about it, you do control your own thoughts. Another advice recommended is to try humor. Find some humor in any event and if there is none, find something to laugh at. It is said that, *"Humor is a cure-all-negative-thoughts medicine".* To better manage our time we need healthy, positive habits and attitudes.

Take some time to think of some of those important things in your life. What is your attitude to them? Jot down the changes you will begin to make as of now.

5 IMPORTANT THINGS	ATTITUDE & CHANGES

"The remarkable thing is, we have a choice
everyday regarding the attitude we will embrace
for that day."
(Charles R. Swindoll)

Chapter 10

Planning Tools #1

*"People often complain about lack of time when
the lack of direction is the real problem."*
(Zig Ziglar)

Planning Tools

In chapter 3, planning and preparation is mentioned as a system or *"generation"* of time. However, if time management is to be simply a way of life, a chapter specifically dealing with planning is vital to attaining success. Of all the planning tools, there are two simple ones which usually generate productive, time-saving results. In this chapter we will consider the first tool, and in the following chapter we will look at the second one.

The dictionary defines planning as *"To formulate a scheme or program for the accomplishment, enactment or attainment of"*; or *"To have a specific aim or purpose".* Answers.com defines it as, *"A scheme, program, or method worked out beforehand for the accomplishment of an objective".* If our objective is to successfully manage our time, then some time spent on planning is fundamental to realising it.

Write your definition for *"planning".*

_____

_____

_____

_____

Planning Tool #1

When I think of planning, I am looking ahead into the future, deciding what I want, and brainstorming the options I have to consider in order to get it. I will then identify and choose the actions that would help me to arrive at my destination. To develop a plan I always find the famous author, Rudyard Kipling's poem a useful technique. He wrote:

"I keep six honest serving men
(They taught me all I knew);
Their names are What and Why and When
And How and Where and Who.
I send them over land and sea,
I send them east and west;
But after they have worked for me,
I give them all a rest".

This poem is a fantastic tool as it leads to open questioning and is actually that checklist I wrote about earlier, which allows you to actively communicate clearly and comprehensively. It ensures that you get all the information you need to make the right choices.

It was Zig Ziglar who said, *"You need a plan to build a house. To build a life, it is even more important to have a plan or goal".* A plan then is really a map or a blueprint which guides us to achieve our goals. Let us walk through an example of the *"six honest serving men"* for a better understanding.

Example: I am going to plan my flight from Port of Spain to New York

Question: **WHAT** is to be done in relation to goals, results and objectives?

Answer: I have to safely operate a flight from Port of Spain to New York.

Question: **WHY** am I doing this?

Answer: I am scheduled to do so, it is my job.

Question: **WHEN** will I go to New York?

Answer: I will go to New York, today as my roster indicates.

Question: **WHERE** will you perform your duties?

Answer: I will perform them on board the aircraft, during the designated flying time.

Question: **WHO** will assist you?

Answer: The other cabin attendants who are also scheduled for this flight.

Question: **HOW** will you do it?

Answer: I will follow the service routine which stipulates exactly what is required for the safe operation of this flight.

Now you identify a goal and plan to accomplish it by using Mr. Kipling's six honest horsemen: *"What; Why; When; Where; Who and How."*

_____

_____

_____

_____

_____

_____

_____

_____

_____

_____

_____

_____

_____

_____

_____

_____

"*Plan your work for today and every day,*
then work your plan."
(Norman Vincent Peale)

Chapter 11

Planning Tools #2

"It is no use saying 'we are doing our best.'
You have got to succeed in doing what
is necessary."
(Winston Churchill)

Planning Tools #2

The second tool which is also quite useful is what I call a quick reference monthly guide/planner. Creating and using this tool is relatively easy and it is instrumental in helping us keep one step ahead. It actually works as an aide memory/reminder.

During my tenure as the in-flight manager, one of the first things I did was to introduce this tool to my staff. I bought a large calendar about three feet by two feet. Then, one month at a time, my staff and I entered as much relevant information as we had available, to remind us of pending required actions and/or recurring tasks, on the available calendar days. We used colours and symbols to reinforce these messages. Then we chose an ideal spot on the wall to hang this calendar, which was easily visible at a quick glance to all of us every day. Any new information was added if and when needed.

To paint a clearer picture, here are some examples of what we did. Instead of waiting until stocks ran out we put in reminders of times to reorder on specific dates. A first aid supply was supported by an image of a red cross. Ordering water was identified at a glance by three blue waves. One of the most important items was the green dollar sign which signified that it was time to begin processing the relevant information to send to payroll, so that the crew could get their foreign exchange subsistence in time. Since public holidays had a major impact on this particular exercise the green dollar signs were critical in helping us stay on target.

As simple a tool as this quick reference was, and because it occupied such an ideal space on the wall for everyone to see – at a glance – it helped us to all keep our eyes on the ball and deliver on time. I use a calendar on my kitchen wall to help me remember both trivial and important dates. Other organisations utilise white boards and similar tools to keep them ahead of the competition.

Other organisations utilise white boards and similar tools to keep them ahead of the competition.

Exercise

In the calendar month below, put in as much information as you can – from birthdays, to picking up the dry cleaning to appointments – anything that you believe is necessary which would serve as reminders and help you to better manage your time.

"Seize the day. Put no trust in the morrow".
(Horace)

Sunday	Monday	Tuesday	Wednesday	Thursday	Friday	Saturday
1	2	3	4	5	6	7
8	9	10	11	12	13	14
15	16	17	18	19	20	21
22	23	24	25	26	27	28
29	30	31	•	•	•	•

January **2012**

Chapter 12

Prioritising with the 80/20 Rule

"I learned that we can do anything, but we can't do everything... at least not at the same time. So think of your priorities not in terms of what activities you do, but when you do them. Timing is everything."
(Dan Millman)

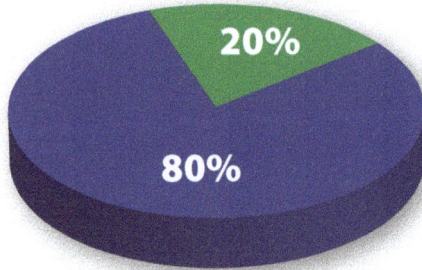

Prioritising with the 80/20 Rule

The dictionary's definition for prioritising is *"to organise according to importance"*, or *"to arrange and deal with in order of importance"*. Despite our abilities to effectively manage our time, we will at times not be able to accomplish everything we would like to. This means there will be times when we have to decide which tasks to complete as opposed to which ones we will not. Prioritising these tasks is the only way forward. How can we then establish which ones are more important than the others?

In setting priorities it is helpful to understand the Pareto Principle which is based on the 80/20 Rule. In 1906, an Italian economist, Vilfredo Pareto, invented a mathematical formula to illustrate the unequal distribution of wealth in his country. He explained that twenty percent of the people owned eighty percent of the wealth. In the 1940's Dr. Joseph M. Juran contended that this ratio could be applied to any scenario, with 80% representing trivial and unimportant things and the 20% symbolising the important and vital things. Even though this was not quite what Pareto intended, Dr. Juran named his conjecture the Pareto's Principle or Pareto's Law.

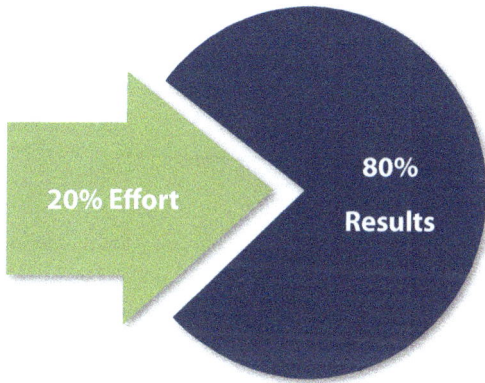

Despite the labeling of this 80/20 theory, we can apply this hypothesis to help us prioritise the many things we have to do on a daily basis. Simply put, if we spend 20% of our time on important activities we would get 80% results because the 80% of time we spend on trivial activities will only result in 20% results. The value of the Pareto Principle is that it allows us to focus on the 20% that really matters which will produce the 80% of results. C. Ray Johnson, in one of the final chapters of his book *CEO Logic : How to Think and Act Like a Chief*

Executive, summarises: *"Prioritising is the answer to time management problems - not computers, efficiency experts, or matrix scheduling. You do not need to do work faster or to eliminate gaps in productivity to make better use of your time. You need to spend more time on the right things..."*

To be able to effectively prioritise we need to first know what we want the outcome to be. We then have to identify what we need to do to get the significant results. In addition, it is important to identify our strengths and weaknesses and focus on how to improve our weaknesses and to maximise our strengths, not only at work, but also in our private lives. It is only after doing this that we can move on to allocating more time on the important activities and reduce the time we spend on less important ones. When we have absolutely no doubt about what our objectives are we can then establish clear priorities.

I used this theory sometimes to assist flight crews during classroom training when I wanted to reinforce the significance of *"putting first things first"*. For example, when faced with an emergency situation which required that the passengers be evacuated, prioritising the steps to follow was crucial. Therefore before opening any exit, it was of paramount importance that the crew member assess the conditions outside the aircraft. The reason for this was to ensure that there was no fire or debris outside to endanger the passengers or puncture the slide which was their only safe way out. By focusing on the 20% that really matters at a time like this, we would be able to save lives and prevent injuries.

So too, Pareto's Principle or the 80/20 Rule can assist us on a daily basis to concentrate on the 20 percent of our work that really matters, to produce the 80% results. After all we don't just want to *"work smart",* we want to work smart on the right things. If the centre of our attention is on the important things, we will surely be well on our way to embracing success.

To effectively prioritise one should:

1. *"In any situation identify the key results to be achieved"*

2. *"Allocate time to deal with productive activities and important issues."*

Chapter 13

The Pareto Principle and the Roles We Play

"It is your destiny to play an infinity
of roles…"
(Deepak Chopra)

The Pareto Principle and the roles we play

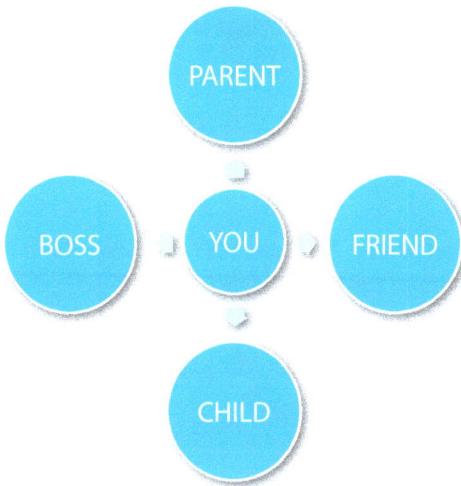

In our daily lives we play many roles, which we interchange without much thought.

For example, even though I may have to behave as a parent to my daughter, I also have to behave as a daughter to my mother. I have to change my role accordingly when I interact with my daughter and my mother. Can you imagine what would happen if I didn't switch roles? Another example is working closely with a friend as a boss and expecting the role of friendship to continue there. It is all well and good to have a good friend to work with. However a professional relationship is the only acceptable one in that scenario and you have to clearly differentiate the roles to succeed. Whenever I think of the many roles we play, I think of William Shakespeare's famous quote;

"All the world's a stage,

And all the men and women merely players:

They have their exits and their entrances,

And one man in his time plays many parts."

But it is the confusion of these many *"parts"* that allows us to lose sight of the importance of these. When we confuse them we then find ourselves often looking for extra time to cope with the result of our actions. How can we fix this?

Exercise #1:

Write down some of the roles you play which are important to you. List one thing next to each role that you can do to improve that role. This should show you the areas where you need to make changes in how you spend your time. For instance, if an important area in your life is quality time with your family as a parent, and next to that role you have written down that you need to have time to do homework with your children, then you will have to reschedule your timetable to fit that specific homework time. In other words making homework priority time will allow you to fit it into that important 20% of your time, which is spent on achieving the important results.

ROLES	CHANGES

It is important to restate that many of our objectives in the important areas of our individual lives can certainly be accomplished if we focus on them. The value of the Pareto Principle is that it allows us to focus on the 20% that really matters and this will produce the 80% of results.

Exercise #2:

Choose a normal day in your life, preferably a Monday, and itemise the things you have to do at work. Using the 80/20 rule identify the 20% which will give you 80% of the results you need. This will be the important things you have prioritised. Now make a second list of the activities you have to do at home. Once again apply the 80/20 rule as you did before. By clearly noting the important results you want, this will ensure that you make time to get them. It's kind of like working backwards or, to again quote Stephen Covey, *"Begin with the end in mind."*

Work Activities

_____

_____

_____

_____

_____

_____

_____

_____

_____

_____

_____

_____

_____

_____

Home Activities

_____

_____

_____

_____

_____

_____

_____

_____

_____

_____

_____

_____

_____

_____

"The essence of the best thinking in the area of time management can be captured in a single phrase: Organise and execute around priorities."
(Stephen Covey)

Chapter 14

Delegation

"The best executive is the one who has sense enough to pick good men to do what he wants done, and self-restraint enough to keep from meddling with them while they do it."

(Theodore Roosevelt)

Delegation

Write a short definition for delegation.

_____
_____
_____
_____

Three other definitions are:

1. *"Appointing a person to act on one's behalf"*

2. *"The process of passing certain tasks and duties from one person to another, typically a superior to a subordinate, the delegate receives sufficient authority to complete the work but the delegator retains the overall responsibility for its success or failure"*

3. *"The entrusting of authority, power and responsibility to another"*

Letting go the reins and handing them over to someone else can be pretty scary, especially since many of us believe that *"I am the only person who can really do this well".* Therefore countless occasions present themselves when we lose out on saving a considerable amount of time by not delegating some tasks. Delegation simply defined is really *"getting work done through others".* Why we do not take full advantage of this golden opportunity is mind boggling.

Author Mark H. McCormack wrote, *"Delegation is the process of building up people, then letting go of a responsibility. It sounds easy, but it almost never is. Egos get in the way. People would rather be perceived as the authority than support the authority or expertise of the people who work for them. It is the ability to delegate which, more than anything else, separates the good managers from the bad ones".* Delegation frees up our time and gives us more elbow room to do those more important things. At the same time it relieves the pressure of having too many things to do in too little time. Remember, when we delegate we are assigning a task we would normally do. In addition, once we have delegated an assignment we have given someone the authority and freedom to do it and we do not have to stand over them or *"breathe down their neck"* while they work.

If not properly executed, delegation can cause you exasperation and discourage and confuse your staff. Therefore if you want to get it right you must first acknowledge that it is not just telling others what to do. Before you delegate you must consider how much autonomy you will give to an individual. You can only decide this by examining both your staff's eagerness and competence. A person can be quite capable of doing a task, but lacks the enthusiasm to want to do it. On the other hand, another may lack some skills but is confident enough to want to tackle the job. There will even be people who are both competent and really keen to do the assigned task. It is therefore important that before you delegate you assess each individual's ability and readiness and be of the same mind with regard to the check points throughout the assignment. You should determine at all times the individual's comfort levels and willingness to undertake any delegated tasks. By all means, take the time to discuss with your staff exactly how much support they will need, so you can correctly determine how much of their free will they can utilise.

Delegation is an incredible tool which, if done correctly, can add hours to your day. Therefore the following points are crucial to embracing success.

Important Points:

🕐 The objectives of the undertaking must be clearly explained. This means that the individual assigned the task must have a clear picture of the intended outcome.

🕐 The person delegated the responsibility must not only be competent and capable but must also be willing to tackle the job.

🕐 You must articulate clear instructions regarding the timing and certainly give as much time as necessary.

🕐 Additionally, inform them that you will be available for support – and be there!

🕐 Identify the strengths and weaknesses of your staff members in order to decide how much independence to give them. Some people may be very proficient; requiring little or no assistance from you, and others will require some more guidance and check points.

🕐 Do not delegate delicate or contentious issues. Give up some stuff you really enjoy doing.

🕐 Remember that even though someone else is doing some of your tasks, the accountability and responsibility of the allocated project remains with YOU.

It is vital that you always recognise and reward the efforts and /or *"good job".*

Everyone wins with delegation. You win because you get additional time to do other things. Your staff in return gains confidence and improves their skills and competencies. Delegation is how we can leverage or control our time effectively. As the manager of the in-flight department I was responsible for approximately four hundred and fifty cabin attendants who really were mostly an absent work force. The only physical time we shared was during our training sessions when there was scheduled classroom time. I had, however, six supervisors and some administrative staff to help me, and at times, I would delegate some of my responsibilities to my supervisors. I would sometimes brief and prepare them to attend meetings with senior management on my behalf. As nervous as this made them feel initially, they tackled it head-on. So not only did I give them *"prime time with the elephants",* I was at the same time ensuring that when I was unavailable, the work went on. To a large extent succession planning was also being done. The benefits of delegation far outweigh any disadvantages. I have listed a few below.

Benefits of Delegation

- You can now concentrate on doing other important things.

- It motivates your staff, enhances their work and helps to build team spirit.

- It develops your staff's capabilities and skills.

- It increases morale, self-confidence and commitment.

- New ideas and more creativity create a more productive team.

- You look good – as a manager!

What are you waiting for then? Go out there and delegate!

Exercise

Think of at least two things each at work and at home that you can delegate and to whom it can be delegated. Remember to consider the individual's capabilities and readiness before you choose how much independence to give to them.

At Work:

1. _____
   _____

2. _____
   _____

At Home:

1. _____
   _____

2. _____
   _____

"Tell me and I forget. Teach me and I remember.
Involve me and I learn."
(Benjamin Franklin)

Chapter 15

Communication

> *"Courage is what it takes to stand up and speak; courage is also what it takes to sit down and listen."*
> (Winston Churchill)

Communication

In the previous chapter the first important point in delegation was; *"The objectives of the undertaking must be clearly explained. This means that the individual assigned the task must have a clear picture of the intended outcome."* For delegation to be successful you must first be able to articulate clear instructions and share pertinent information. Communication is vital to avoid mistakes and not waste valuable time. After all, if the person to whom you have delegated a task has a vague or ambiguous understanding of the expected results, then the purpose of delegating would have been defeated. Two definitions for communication are:

"*The means through which people exchange feelings and ideas with each other*"

"*The transfer/exchange of information and the understanding of that information, from one person to another*"

Despite those simple enough meanings, we need to pause and consider how communication impacts on our time.

Before you even begin to speak the communication process has already started. Your brain draws on past experience you have had with this individual and because of this awareness, a certain level of comfort or uneasiness may be felt. This may lead to assumptions and misconceptions and if not verbally corrected the transaction can end in abject failure.

Because we listen with both our ears and eyes, body language and tone of voice can alter the message. Regarding communication, research shows that:

In communicating when using the telephone:

"*Words account for 18%*" and

"*Intonation for 82%*"

However in communicating face to face according to research, these percentages change to:

RECEIVER	SENDER
What you hear = 40% of the message	Tone of voice; Vocal clarity; Verbal expressiveness
What you see or feel = 50% of the message	Facial expression; Dress & Grooming; Posture (body language); Eye contact; Touch; Gesture
Words = 10% of the message	Words

Amazing isn't it? Words account for only 10% of what we hear in a direct conversation. Other research alters this formula slightly to:

- *"Words account for 7%*
- *Intonation for 38% and*
- *Body Language accounts for 55%"*

Do you remember Pareto's principle? Author Jim Rohn wrote, *"Effective communication is 20% what you know and 80% how you feel about what you know."*

The simple model below can help to explain that communication is always a two-way process.

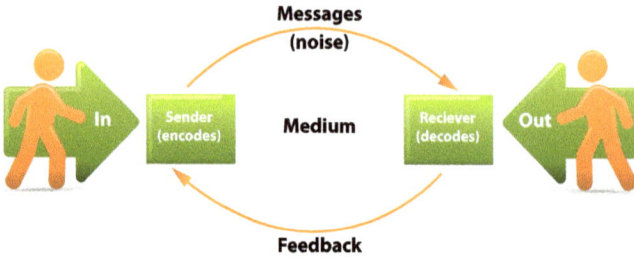

According to the above communication model there are two key ingredients, namely the message and feedback, necessary for effective communication.

Message

From the sender to the receiver is the message which has to be interpreted by the receiver. Despite choosing the right words and the best medium, other distractions can occur to distort and obscure the message. Some of these are:

- Emotions
- Noises
- Prejudices
- Speed over clarity
- Interpretation
- Physical distractions
- Accents
- Assumptions
- Status
- Body language
- Health
- Education

Face to face communication is a wonderful way to build rapport and ensure that the non-verbal actions or body language are in sync with the spoken words. If the sender's non-verbal actions contradict his words, the receiver will become quite confused. During my days of working on the aircraft my inability to clearly communicate with a passenger who spoke a foreign language negatively affected the process. Luckily because we were face to face, I was able to supplement my words with signs. I could then use these actions to cross that communication language barrier. There are other ways to break through the many communication barriers, assuming we are open to other thoughts and ideas. The next chapter covers some of these ways.

Feedback

In order to give feedback the receiver must listen and understand exactly what the sender has said. To demonstrate that you are listening you give your full and undivided attention. Clear your mind of everything else and, if face to face, maintain eye contact. By doing this you will also be showing your interest non-verbally. If you are not clear on what you have heard, please summarise or rephrase what you heard for confirmation. It is super important to respond with empathy to display your genuine concern and understanding. Put yourself in the other person's *"shoes"* and feel and share his thoughts and emotions.

It is only when both the sender and the receiver are on the same *"wave length"* that communication is effective and successful.

"Calvin: Sometimes when I'm talking, my words can't keep up with my thoughts. I wonder why we think faster than we speak.

Hobbes: Probably so we can think twice."
(Bill Watterson, Calvin & Hobbes)

Chapter 16

Breaking the Communication
Barriers # 1 VAK

"The problem with communication is the illusion that it has occurred."

(George Bernard Shaw)

Breaking the Communication Barriers # 1- VAK

Do you sometimes feel when talking to someone that you are talking to a wall? If communication is so simple why do we often find it so challenging? Let us explore some research done in the early 1970's to help us overcome the many barriers we often encounter when we converse.

Richard Bandler and John Grinder developed a model called, the Neuro-Linguistic Programming Model (NLP). It was designed to increase our self awareness and so change how we relate to others. According to this model, how our brains interpret and deal with what we hear depends on our five senses of sight, sound, touch, taste and smell. However, the three which are most prevalent for this mental processing are, sight (visual), sound (auditory) and touch (kinesthetic). The other two of taste and smell are closely associated and less significant in the process. The NLP model states that there are therefore three major learning styles, namely: Visual, Auditory and Kinesthetic or VAK. It contends that we will each assimilate knowledge and information depending on which sense is individually most predominant and as a result each learns differently. This in turn will have a major impact on effective communication between different learners. A better understanding of these styles may help us to remove some of our communication *"walls"*.

Visual people learn best by looking at things. Their learning is stimulated by seeing graphs, charts, pictures, faxes, memos, videos etc. During classroom sessions I sometimes used videos to reinforce emergency training for flight attendants. By looking at them many crew members quickly grasped the significance of the main ideas. After all, *"A picture paints a thousand words".* The NLP model recommends that when talking to Visuals you reinforce the message by showing them pictures, letters and even sketching a diagram to illustrate what you're saying. Using phrases like: *"I see your point." "I want you to look at this." "Am I painting a clear picture?"* to a Visual person helps to facilitate the communication process.

People with an auditory style learn best when they can hear the information being presented such as in conversations, discussions, voice mail, audio tapes and phone calls. Auditory individuals generally talk a lot and like to hear the sound of their own voices. It is important to listen to them and allow them to have their say. To better interact with an auditory person, the NLP model advises to use phrases like: *"I hear what you're saying"; "I want to make this loud and clear"; "Does what I am saying sound right to you?"* Using these aural expressions with auditory people give them an instant understanding of what you are saying.

Individuals with a kinesthetic style will rely on the sense of touch or feelings. For example, they must *"feel"* comfortable to conduct business with you. Persons with this style generally feel their way through life. They must mentally connect to their environment. They are very responsive to body tension, physical proximity to others and movement. To effectively communicate with a Kinesthetic, the phrases suggested to use are: *"I feel that I'm in touch with what you're saying." "I want you to get a grasp of this." "Do you have a handle on this?"* The relation to touch or feelings helps them to **feel** better and clinches it for them.

It is a good idea to discover what our individual learning style is and make an effort to recognise those styles of others to help remove some of the communication barriers. It is said that using auditory language on a Kinesthetic or vice versa would be like trying to mix oil and water, it just doesn't work. Psychologist and business guru, Anthony Robbins, summed it up brilliantly when he said, *"To effectively communicate, we must realise that*

Learning Styles

 Visual

 Kinesthetic

 Auditory

we are all different in the way we perceive the world and use this understanding as a guide to our communication with others".

Exercise

Take some time now to write down your preferred style: _____

_____
_____
_____
_____
_____

Think of three specific people:

1. _____

2. _____

3. _____

Identify barriers you may have experienced with them:

_____
_____
_____
_____
_____
_____

_____

_____

_____

_____

_____

Consider adapting the VAK model when next you communicate with them:

1._____

2._____

3._____

Discovering others preferred learning styles and meeting them there will certainly help to remove some barriers and improve how you communicate with others.

"The way we communicate with others and with ourselves ultimately determines the quality of our lives."

(Anthony Robbins)

Chapter 17

Breaking the
Communication Barrier # 2
– The Ladder of Inference

"Communication works for those who work at it".
(John Powell)

Breaking the Communication Barrier # 2 – The Ladder of Inference

Understanding our *"Ladder of Inference"* can also help us understand how we make assumptions and will help us decide on our next course of action, which can sometimes create barriers. The Ladder of Inference was developed by Chris Argyris and subsequently presented in Peter Senge's book *"The Fifth Discipline Field book".*

Diagram of *"The Ladder of Inference"*

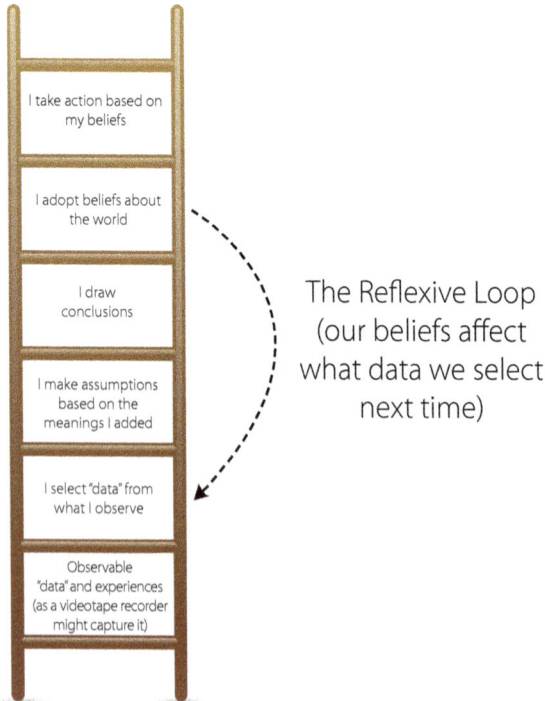

I take action based on my beliefs

I adopt beliefs about the world

I draw conclusions

I make assumptions based on the meanings I added

I select "data" from what I observe

Observable "data" and experiences (as a videotape recorder might capture it)

The Reflexive Loop (our beliefs affect what data we select next time)

It describes the thinking process that we go through usually without realising it, to get from a fact to a decision or action. It is based on *"our commitment to our beliefs once made".* That is, we make assumptions or draw conclusions from what we see together with our past experiences, then we act. The following references from *"The Fifth Discipline"* by Peter Senge help to explain this process.

"In essence to climb the ladder:

We start with real observable data.

We add meanings and make assumptions based on the meaning added to that data.

We draw conclusions and make decisions based on our assumptions.

Then we take action based upon those conclusions and assumptions."

It is important to grasp that this move up the ladder happens almost in an instant. It continues to reoccur all day long, when we interact with people, read the news, etc. We observe a situation, apply our filters and assumptions and reach a conclusion – then we act on our conclusions. Bear in mind, though, that other people after climbing their own ladder all day long arrive at their own conclusions also.

Have you ever been accused of putting two and two together and making five? Have you ever jumped to the wrong conclusion? We are usually under pressure to act now, rather than spend time to reason things out or think things through about the true facts. Not only will this lead to a wrong conclusion but it can cause conflict with people who have drawn quite different conclusions on the same matter. This negatively affects how we communicate.

Understanding the ladder of inference helps us to suspend judgment until we have all the facts.

The experts recommend that to increase your awareness of the ladder of inference:

⏰ *"Become more aware of your own reasoning and thinking. Remember others make legitimate inferences and assessments of the same situations.*

⏰ *Become curious and try to empathise and see it from their perspectives.*

⏰ *Reveal your data and reasoning to them so that they can also understand it from your point of view.*

⏰ *Be willing to admit to mistakes." (Unknown)*

While others may not always agree with you, they will be able to see how you reached your conclusions. You will also be able in turn to understand how they arrived at theirs. At the end of the day, it will then be alright to even agree to disagree and effective communication would have taken place. Remember *"Communication is a skill that you can learn. It's like riding a bicycle or typing. If you're willing to work at it, you can rapidly improve the quality of every part of your life."* (Brian Tracy)

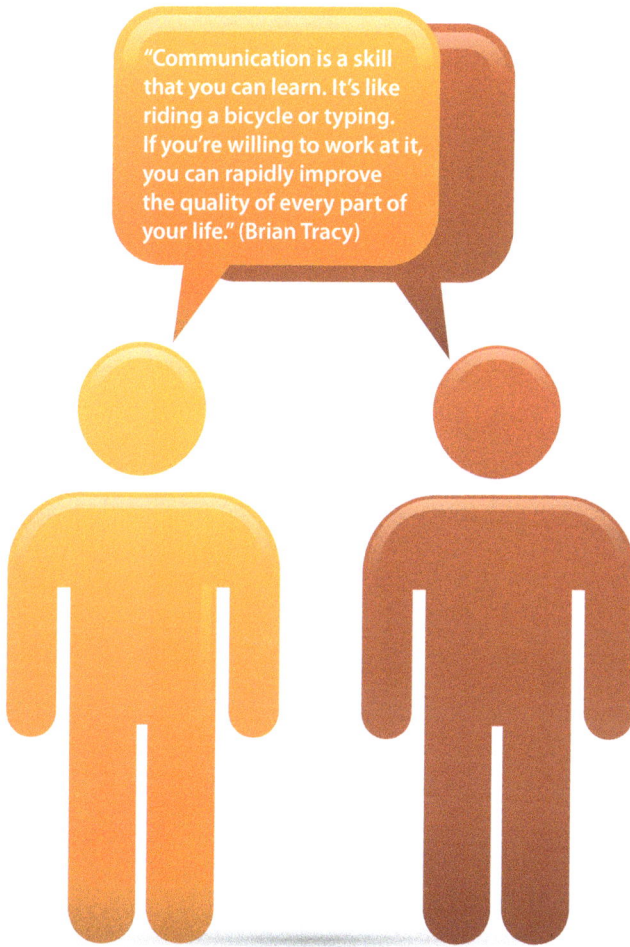

*"If there is any great secret of success in life,
it lies in the ability to put yourself in the other
person's place and to see things from his point of
view as well as your own."*
(Henry Ford)

Chapter 18

Time Wasters - Personal

> *"A man who dares to waste one hour of life has not discovered the value of life."*
> **(Charles Darwin)**

Time Wasters

TIME
WASTERS

Eliminating and Reducing Time Wasters

We all have the same amount of time and it must be spent at the rate of sixty seconds in every minute. Yet we are all guilty of wasting time because it is a human failing. Some wasted time can be justified as being constructive because it may help to relax or reduce tension. If it is done by choice and is not a failing, then that's okay. Other wasted time, however, can be quite frustrating. We are personally responsible for wasting our time and there will be occasions when we even have to manage how other people and/or events impact on our time. Without a doubt, whether it is personal or public (other people), plugging these annoying time leakages will certainly boost both our private and professional productivity. Let us identify and explore some ways to avoid some of these irritations especially as it relates to the workplace.

Personal Time Wasters

Procrastination

Procrastination comes from the Latin word for *"tomorrow"* and is the number one greatest time waster. It is also known as *"the thief of time".* A dictionary definition for it is, *"to put off that which seems unappealing".* I once read that, *"Successful people do not procrastinate, especially in matters they know are important to them. As someone has rightly said, people don't fail because they intend to fail. They fail because they fail to do what they intend to do."* I could not have said it any better.

Why do we procrastinate?

- Some of us do it because it has become a habit to do so.
- Others may feel insecure and by doubting their abilities they postpone taking action.
- It may be, too, that if doing something brings with it anxiety or discomfort, some will steer clear of doing the task.
- Avoiding facing guilty feelings caused by procrastination will also lead others to continue to sidestep activities.

However, once we acknowledge why as individuals we drag our feet, we can begin to *"fix"* us. Whether we use checklists or organisers we will have to prioritise our activities, categorise them by how important and urgent they are, and then actually do them based on their rankings. It is a good idea not to overdo it. If you break big tasks into smaller ones, it will be much easier to set a comfortable pace and accomplish all of them. To tackle any anxiety issues, take deep breaths and then just do the chosen tasks! Remember to also reward yourself. Having scheduled downtime will help you to focus on getting things done to be able to enjoy your leisure time.

Crises

If we procrastinate this could lead to a crisis; therefore do not delay doing important things. In addition some crises may occur because of circumstances beyond our control. For example, unrealistic deadlines, last minute changes, mistakes/errors, and machinery which breaks down can lead to disasters. To handle these predicaments:

- Review past ones and look for patterns so that you can develop ways to address recurring problems.

- Contingency planning helps

- Breathe deeply, objectively consider what needs to be done, the alternatives available, prioritise and deal effectively with the crisis. After all, you do not want to precipitate another crisis by simply trying to handle the first one.

Disorganisation

You can recognise that you are disorganised when:

⏰ You spend time looking for things because you have forgotten where you have placed them.

⏰ You redo stuff because you forgot something the first time around.

⏰ You do things that need not be done at all.

⏰ Activities take longer because you didn't take the time to inform yourself properly.

⏰ You are unable to find a very important piece of paper.

The best advice I got to mitigate disorganisation is to keep things where you can find them. Not necessarily neat – order means knowing where things are. Remember the famous expression, *"A place for everything, and everything in its place".* In the aviation field, being disorganised was definitely not an option. At an altitude of approximately thirty-five thousand feet, we could not easily consider telephoning for extra stores or equipment. Before the aircraft took off we had to check and recheck and organise in such a way to not only have enough supplies but also to store them safely to avoid creating any emergency situations.

Not saying "no"

This time waster is not always easy to deal with but:

⏰ Learn to say no appropriately. For example: *"I am sorry, I wish I could help but unfortunately I can't leave what I'm doing now".*

⏰ Remember it takes you away from your goals and objectives.

⏰ You cannot do it – be firm – sorry I wish I could but I can't.

⏰ You can even delay decisions and promise to do it tomorrow if you have the time.

"It has been my observation that most people get ahead during the time that others waste."

(Henry Ford)

Chapter 19

Time Wasters -
Public Time Wasters

"Short as life is, we make it still shorter by the careless waste of time."

(Victor Hugo)

Public Time Wasters

It is all well and good to be responsible for the time we personally waste. We have to also be cognizant of the influence of others as it impacts on our time.

Drop-in visitors

Controlling visitors requires courtesy and judgment. You can:

⏰ Limit the number of people you invite to your work area.

⏰ Go to meet a colleague at his work area.

⏰ Don't invite them to sit – this usually shortens the visit.

⏰ Be honest and explain that you will have to be excused since you are doing something extremely important.

Unproductive meetings

Results of a poorly planned meeting include:

⏰ Mixed messages

⏰ Unclear goals and strategies

⏰ A random list of things to do afterwards

⏰ Lack of results, which lead to another time-consuming fruitless meeting

To avoid these, meetings must be planned and timed with an agenda to brief/prepare everyone and then to keep them focused and on target. Minutes should list actions expected by whom, when, and reporting-back dates. Bear in mind that others also have their personal activities needing attention and that time is also important to them.

Telephone calls

Limit these by:

⏰ Providing short answers and avoiding small talk.

⏰ Have someone else answer your calls; you can review which ones need a personal follow-up and which ones can be delegated.

⏰ Having achieved its business purpose, very politely end the telephone conversation.

Mail

⏰ Sort into information and action

⏰ Use the telephone, e-mail or fax to respond promptly.

⏰ Write a brief note on the original document and take action immediately. (Make an additional copy if needed). I used this method a lot as the manager of the in-flight department, since being such a large department, it really helped to accelerate how tasks were done.

Waiting for someone

Regarding appointments and meetings:

⏰ Request the assistant to call when meeting is ready and return to your office

⏰ Reschedule if possible

⏰ Use time constructively – read mail, develop plans or write letters

Additionally do not keep people waiting because you are the boss. That only demonstrates that you are inconsiderate and disrespectful of their time.

Computer games & surfing the internet - (Personal & Public)

Be wary of this and guard against it. Remember staff look for reasons to justify their time spent doing this.

In life we may not always achieve all we set out to but many of our objectives in the important areas of our individual lives can be met if we can honestly identify why we indulge in time wasters and then make a conscious decision to address our shortcomings.

List other time wasters and ways to avoid them:

_____

_____

_____

_____

_____

_____

"Willful waste brings woeful want."
(Thomas Fuller)

Chapter 20

Time Savers/Tips

"A stitch in time saves nine."
(Proverb)

Time Savers/Tips

Technology can save you time. For example:

- Telephone enhancements – answering machines; dialing features; hands-free operation and call forwarding
- Voice mail
- Call diversion
- Pagers

- Mobile phones

- E-mail

- Facsimile transmissions

- Alternatives to meetings – conference calls; teleconferencing (tying two or more meetings together); video conferencing

- Computer enhancements – portable, scanners, modems, electronic notepads; electronic organisers; speech recognisers; flash drives

Here is a simple example how technology helped us when operating flights. The Lockheed 1011 aircraft had a capacity for at least two hundred and fifty passengers. It was designed with an intercom system which allowed communication from the front, middle and the rear of the aircraft. Therefore instead of walking all the way from the back to the front of the cabin to ask a question, we simply used the intercom system. It was also used by the captain to keep all of us informed at the same time. Additionally, using an emergency code, he could alert all crew members simultaneously that something was amiss.

Reducing Paper

Despite these wonderful hi-tech tools that make our work easier and save us time, do they actually lessen the amount of paper that we deal with? We have all heard about the myth of the paperless office. If we can communicate by phones and e-mail, etc., why have we built paper into our way of working, whether it is necessary or not? List three reasons why we keep paper.

1. _____
   _____

2. _____
   _____

3. _____
   _____

   Possible answers may be:

- To use as a reference

- It is interesting

- It's significant to your work

- No particular reason – it has always been kept

- The company insists on three copies of everything

- It might come in handy

- To read when you find time

- As a safety measure

Some Tips for reducing paper

- Accept that no office is going to be completely paperless

- Automate – pay bills etc. on line

- Secure financial and legal records
- File it, pass it on, action it or dispose of it
- Keep your desk uncluttered
- Keep only the necessary papers on hand
- Use a simple filing system
- Use a shredder to get rid of paper
- Use both sides of the paper
- Ask yourself – Do I need to print this?
- Print one copy and pass it around or put it on a notice board
- Collect scrap and use it as note paper

List other ways that you can reduce paper:

_____

_____

_____

_____

Having to constantly sort through papers can rob you of hours which could be better utilised during your day. By reducing paper you can actually save that time for other important matters. As a bonus remember that reducing paper will also have a positive effect on the environment.

"Your greatest asset is your earning ability.
Your greatest resource is
your time."
(Brian Tracy)

Chapter 21

Dreams

"I have a dream today."
(Dr. Martin Luther King)

Dreams

You may be wondering why I chose to write a chapter on dreams. After all what does this have to do with successful time management? It was the American philosopher, Henry David Thoreau who wrote, *"If one advances confidently in the direction of one's dreams, and endeavors to live the life which one has imagined, one will meet with a success unexpected in common hours".* I could not have explained it better. Our dreams can have a positive impact on how we manage our time if we *"grasp the nettle"* and pursue them. There are many synonyms for the word, *"dream".*

Ten of them are:
1. Envisage
2. Delight
3. Imagine
4. Fantasize
5. Hope
6. Desire
7. Goal
8. Wish
9. Aspiration
10. Vision

Write down which one is your favorite even if it is not on the above list. _____

I once read that *"Dreams are like the paints of a great artist. Your dreams are your paint; the world is your canvas. Believing is the brush that converts your dreams into a masterpiece of reality."* Dreaming is also free, so there is absolutely no reason for each and every one of us to not have castles in the sky. It was Bernard Edmonds who eloquently stated:

"To dream anything that you want to dream

That's the beauty of the human mind

To do anything that you want to do

That is the strength of the human will

To trust yourself to test your limits

That is the courage to succeed."

What this means, is that at the end of the day it all begins with a dream. If we envisage what we want to accomplish in a specific time frame, it is our belief in ourselves which will push us to persevere and thrive. If we genuinely want to succeed at time management then we have to not only dream but have the guts and the determination to develop healthier habits and use the tools in the previous chapters to help us reach that goal. Easier said than done, I know, but it is most certainly within reach.

Take the time now to write down one of your dreams; then list the things you will have to do to turn that one dream into reality.

_____

_____

_____

_____

_____

_____

_____

_____

_____

_____

_____

_____

_____

_____

_____

_____

_____

_____
_____
_____
_____
_____
_____
_____
_____
_____
_____
_____
_____

"All men dream, but not equally. Those
who dream by night in the dusty recesses of
their minds wake in the day to find that it
was vanity; but the dreamers of the day are
dangerous men, for they may act their dreams
with open eyes, to make it possible."
(T.E. Lawrence)

Conclusion

"Time waits for no one."
(Credited to Mick Jagger
and Keith Richards)

"Time Waits for No One" is the title of a song by the British rock and roll band, the Rolling Stones, from its 1974 album; It's Only Rock 'n' Roll. If this expression is true and I'm sure we will have no arguments here to dispute it, we are then obliged to value every moment we have. A friend gave me this brilliant poem she came across. It goes like this:

"To realise the value of "one year":
Ask a student who has failed a final exam.

To realise the value of "one month":
Ask a mother who has given birth to a premature baby.

To realise the value of "one week" :
Ask an editor of a weekly newspaper.

To realise the value of "one hour" :
Ask the lovers who are waiting to meet.

To realise the value of "one minute" :
Ask the person who has missed the train, bus or plane.

To realise the value of "one-second" :
Ask a person who has survived an accident.

To realise the value of "one millisecond" :
Ask the person who has won a silver medal in the Olympics."

"Good words and well spoken" as this friend of mine refers to it.

By now we should have achieved our objectives and you should be able to:

- Define time management and be better able to improve your time management skills
- Identify various established systems of time management and choose the one which is ideal for you
- Analyse problems that arise with regard to one's attitude and habits

- Plan and prioritise tasks
- Identify time wasters and learn how to eliminate them
- Better understand how to successfully delegate
- Communicate more effectively
- Acknowledge the benefits of successful time management
- Better manage self and time – and also
- Begin with a dream

We can all embrace success through effective time management and reap a bountiful harvest of extra time. By choosing a system that works for us; by planning, prioritising and separating the important and urgent activities, including reducing or better yet eliminating time wasters, we will always have the time available to handle both the expected and unexpected events.

We do not have to become fantastic jugglers managing events and activities. Remember the garden? Own it. It's your garden, and long before the flowers bloom or the trees grow, the effort you've put into growing them will result in a healthier garden or taller trees. The more you invest in managing you today, the more you have ensured results of a balanced, well adjusted existence on the morrow. So spend time in your garden, after all it's your life and the end result allows you to embrace success time after time with the priceless treasure of additional golden hours in your days. After all successful time management is simply a way of life.

It is therefore essential to, *"Take time:*

Take time to think – It is the source of all power.

Take time to read – It is the fountain of wisdom.

Take time to play – It is the source of perpetual youth.

Take time to be quiet – It is the opportunity to seek God.

Take time to be aware – It is the opportunity to help others.

Take time to love and be loved – It is God's greatest gift.

Take time to laugh – It is the music of the soul.

Take time to be friendly – It is the road to happiness.

Take time to dream – It is what the future is made of.

Take time to pray – It is the greatest power on earth.

Take time to give – It is too short a day to be selfish.

Take time to work – It is the price of success."

"There is a time for everything…"
(Ecclesiastes 3:1; The Holy Bible)

Index

www.ingramcontent.com/pod-product-compliance
Lightning Source LLC
Chambersburg PA
CBHW051125210326
41520CB00040B/7518